Find Your Future

LIFE AFTER
HIGH SCHOOL

A Teen Guide to
Career Planning

NICHOLAS SUIVSKI

TWENTY-FIRST CENTURY BOOKS / MINNEAPOLIS

Twenty-First Century Books™
An imprint of Lerner Publishing Group, Inc.
241 First Avenue North
Minneapolis, MN 55401 USA

For reading levels and more information, look up this title at www.lernerbooks.com.

Main body text set in Bembo Std Regular.
Typeface provided by Monotype Typography.

Library of Congress Cataloging-in-Publication Data

Names: Suivski, Nicholas, author.
Title: Life after high school : a teen guide to career planning / [Nicholas Suivski].
Description: Minneapolis : Lerner Publications, [2025] I Includes bibliographical
    references and index. I Audience: Ages 11–18 I Audience: Grades 7–9 I Summary:
    "High school students are faced with seemingly endless choices for what life after
    graduation looks like. Explore options for jobs, housing, and further education
    through practical, easy to follow strategies"—Provided by publisher.
Identifiers: LCCN 2023049884 (print) I LCCN 2023049885 (ebook) I
    ISBN 9798765611333 (library binding) I ISBN 9798765630020 (paperback) I
    ISBN 9798765638767 (epub)
Subjects: LCSH: Teenagers—Vocational guidance—Juvenile literature. I High school
    students—Vocational guidance—Juvenile literature.
Classification: LCC HF5381.2 .S8825 2025 (print) I LCC HF5381.2 (ebook) I DDC
    650.140835—dc23/eng/20240207

LC record available at https://lccn.loc.gov/2023049884
LC ebook record available at https://lccn.loc.gov/2023049885

Manufactured in the United States of America
1 – CG – 7/15/24

CONTENTS

INTRODUCTION

It's never too early to set your sights on the road ahead. Where do you want to be two months from today? How about two years from now? Or even 20? Perhaps you want to go to college. Or maybe you want to start your career in a trade right after graduation. Do you know how to get where you want to go? Making smart decisions now and planning your education and career ahead of time will set you on the path to achieving these future goals.

This book is a guide for making smart decisions in high school and getting ready for what comes after. It provides helpful advice, clear steps, and useful tips to make the most of this important time. Start getting ready early, and you'll be well on your way to finding success in college, work, and life after school.

Planning out your education and career means making smart choices about school and work. In this book, we'll explore the benefits of pursuing higher education, the various educational options available, the importance of setting goals,

It's okay to have questions about the future. Finding resources to help you answer them can help you get a head start.

and the value of self-reflection. By adopting smart strategies, you can confidently navigate your journey toward a fulfilling and prosperous future.

CHAPTER ONE
Getting a Head Start in High School

During high school, there are lots of ways you can explore who you are and what you want to do after graduation. From classes and clubs to volunteering, sports, and other extracurricular activities, it might seem like there are endless options to explore your interests. All these experiences can help you create your future, but you probably won't have time to do them all. It is also important to avoid becoming burnt out, or overly fatigued from doing too much without letting your mind and body rest. Knowing which opportunities are open to you now and which spark your curiosity can help you decide which classes and activities are right for you.

Whether you're headed for a career after graduation, college, or something else entirely, the choices you make during high school matter. What you decide to do today can expand your knowledge, open doors for careers, and help you grow as a person. There are more options available to students today than ever before. With a few practical tips, you can design the path that aligns with your needs and aspirations.

High School Diplomas and GEDs

Finishing high school is one of the first and biggest goals you can accomplish to open doors to careers and opportunities. There are two paths you can take: getting a high school diploma or passing the General Educational Development (GED) test.

A high school diploma is an official document that shows you have successfully completed your secondary education. It's usually awarded after you complete all the necessary academic requirements, coursework, and electives in your high school. A high school diploma is often considered a minimum educational

Graduating from high school is a huge accomplishment that can set you up for future success.

qualification for various opportunities, including college admissions and many jobs.

Not everyone is able to finish high school in a traditional manner. Finances, family situations, and other issues can get in the way. The GED is an alternative to a high school diploma. To earn a GED, you take a test on core subjects, including language arts, math, science, and social studies. You can get a GED at any age. Many colleges and employers consider it as valuable as a high school diploma, so you can still apply for financial aid, scholarships, and job opportunities.

Preparing for Higher Education

College diplomas, apprenticeships, and trade school degrees can open doors to new opportunities. As Benjamin Franklin once said, "An investment in knowledge pays the best interest." Whether you're on track to earn a high school diploma or a GED, it's useful to consider whether you want to pursue education beyond a high school level.

Common Educational Paths After High School

There are many educational pathways available for both high school and GED graduates. Read about the following options and think about which ones might be a good fit for you.

- *Community College*: Community colleges offer associate's degree programs and vocational certificates in smaller classes that allow for more personalized attention. Many students start at their local community college before transferring to a university for further studies.

Attending a community college or university gives you an opportunity to learn with people who share your educational goals.

- *University*: Universities offer bachelor's degrees and advanced studies. They have a wide range of academic options, but classes might be larger and tuition may cost more compared to community colleges.
- *Trade School*: Trade and vocational schools are great options for people interested in skilled careers such as electricians, plumbers, or chefs. These programs are focused on specialized career training and provide hands-on learning. They are usually shorter than traditional degrees, getting you ready for job opportunities in less time.
- *Apprenticeship*: Apprenticeships offer a unique way to learn by doing. These programs let you earn money while gaining valuable skills. Industries such as construction and manufacturing often provide apprenticeships

9

that combine on-the-job training with classroom learning so you can earn the credentials required by government or official organizations and more easily apply for full-time jobs.

Academic Preparation for High School Students

If you have an idea of what subjects you like, or an industry you may want to enter, you can take electives in high school that will prepare you for a job in that field. You can also choose to focus on core subjects that build a strong foundation for any career path.

Advanced Placement classes allow high school students to try out college-level work and earn college credits.

The Difference Between AP Courses and Dual Enrollment Programs

Advanced Placement (AP) Courses. AP courses are college-level classes taught in high schools. They are like a taste of college before you graduate. By taking these classes, you show you can handle college-level material while still in high school. At the end of the course, you can take an AP exam. Depending on your exam score, you might get college credit or be placed in higher-level college courses.

Dual Enrollment Programs. With dual enrollment programs, you can take college classes while in high school. It's like being in two places at once! These classes count for both high school and college credits. You can find these classes at community colleges, universities, or online. It's a great way to experience college-level learning and see what college will be like.

Advanced Placement (AP) classes cover college-level material and could earn you college credits before you even enroll in a college or university. Some schools also provide dual enrollment opportunities. Dual enrollment lets you take college classes while in high school, giving you a head start on credits so you can take more classes in college or graduate college early.

Although academics are important, getting involved in extracurricular activities will also help you stand out. Colleges and employers want to see that you've developed skills outside of your studies. You can join clubs or sports teams or volunteer for community service. In clubs, you can take on leadership roles such as club president, vice president, secretary, treasurer, or event coordinator. In sports teams, leadership roles can include team captain, assistant captain, or positions that involve organizing team events and activities. You can also consider starting a new club or community service project, which shows both leadership and initiative.

The key is to show active engagement in the club or activity and take on responsibilities that help in its growth and improvement. Aside from looking good on college and job applications, such roles and experiences will also help you develop important skills that you may need in the future.

Academic Preparation for GED Earners

If a high school diploma is not an option for you, getting your GED can also help you build your existing skills and develop new ones that will help you succeed in the future. As you prepare to take the GED exam, be mindful of the topics you are struggling with. Consider going to a tutoring center to get extra help with those subjects.

Table 1. Tips on Academic Preparation for GED Earners	
Academic Preparation	**Description**
Building on GED Skills	
Transferable Skills	Preparing for the GED test will teach you valuable skills like time management, self-discipline, critical thinking, and problem-solving. These skills are important for further education, no matter what you choose to do next.
Study Habits	The study habits you developed while preparing for the GED test, such as consistent studying, active note-taking, and using different learning techniques, can be applied to further learning in any new setting.
Test-Taking Skills	By studying for the GED exam, you'll improve essential test-taking skills, such as reading for comprehension, managing exam time effectively, and reducing test anxiety.
Addressing Gaps	
Find Your Weaknesses	Are there any subjects that you don't feel as confident about? Reflect on your performance and seek academic advising, or seek assistance from local tutoring centers.
Use Available Resources	Make the most of tutoring centers, study groups, and office hours with instructors. Many colleges offer free tutoring in different subjects to help you succeed.
Take Extra Courses	Consider taking additional courses or workshops to improve specific skills. This can be helpful if your further education demands skills that weren't covered in your GED studies.

Financial Planning

Pursuing higher education can be expensive, and it requires careful financial planning. Seek out information on financial aid options, such as scholarships, grants, and student loans.

Scholarships are based on achievements or talents and don't need to be paid back. Grants help students with financial needs, can come from various sources, and don't need to be paid back. Student loans can cover education costs but must be paid back over time.

Knowing your expenses will keep you financially prepared. Make a financial plan to save money for tuition, books, and living expenses. Use a budget to manage your finances well while in school and after you graduate.

A financial plan can also help to think ahead about the kinds of expenses you will face once your college classes start. As you do, think of ways to cut costs, such as buying used textbooks or finding affordable housing.

Joining the Military After High School

Choosing to join the military after high school is a bold decision that sets you on a different path than traditional work, college, or trade school. It's a chance to grow and prepare for other academic and career opportunities.

The military provides many opportunities for education that can prepare you for careers within and outside of the military. There are many opportunities to gain knowledge and skills in exciting fields such as technology, medicine, and leadership. Service members can get financial aid to pay for higher education, as well as health care and other benefits.

You can also meet people from all walks of life, forming friendships that open your eyes to different cultures and perspectives.

But while the military provides many opportunities, it isn't for everyone. Being in the military has its challenges, and it is important to understand both the rewards and the significant risks associated with service. Many people in the military are sent all over the world, often to areas of conflict. It can be difficult and dangerous work. Not only are there physical dangers of combat, but there are also mental and emotional challenges to consider. Veterans and active service members often face stress and trauma from witnessing or experiencing distressing events. These can sometimes lead to long-term mental health challenges, such as post-traumatic stress disorder (PTSD). You might miss your family and friends from home, and the continuous transitions and relocations can take a toll on personal relationships.

But despite these challenges, many service members find comfort in the bonds they form within the military. Your fellow service members can become a second family, and the sense of purpose you'll gain from serving your country can be incredibly rewarding. If you decide to leave the military, the skills and experiences you've gained will give you a head start in college and future jobs.

During high school, if you're considering joining the military, focus on improving your physical fitness through regular exercise and participating in sports to develop stamina and teamwork. Academically, aim for good grades and consider joining a Reserve Officers' Training Corps (ROTC) program. ROTC is a program offered at many high schools and colleges in the United States. Students enrolled in ROTC prepare to become officers in the US military. Research military branches, connect with recruiters for specific insights, and engage with veterans to gain a firsthand understanding of military life. Join clubs and community projects to improve your leadership and teamwork skills. Uphold strong lifestyle standards and avoid activities that might lead to legal troubles. Stay informed about global military affairs. Remember, joining the military is a significant and often long-term commitment. Make sure it aligns with your values and long-term goals before you enlist.

Factor in Your Personal Needs and Goals

Deciding what path to take after high school is a big decision. It can seem overwhelming or scary. But it can also be exciting. You get to choose the next important step in your life. Do your research and spend time reflecting to make a smart and informed decision that feels right to you. Here are some tips to help you start:

a. *Know your strengths and weaknesses*: Think about what you're good at and enjoy doing. Do you like working with others, or are you most productive alone? Do you like making new things, or are you happiest with a set of instructions? Asking yourself these types of questions will help you choose a path that matches your skills and passions.

b. *Research different careers*: Talk to friends, family, and teachers to learn more about different careers and industries to see which interests you the most. You can make an informed choice once you understand what it's like to work in different fields.

c. *Think about the cost and the return on investment*: Planning for your future is an opportunity to make smart financial choices. Higher education can be expensive, so consider the cost of your chosen path and the potential income it might lead to. If this equation isn't adding up, you can ask a guidance counselor or mentor for their advice.

d. *Listen to your heart*: College might not be the best choice for everyone. It can be expensive, and it's a big-time commitment. Even if your parents or friends want you to do one thing, it's okay to let them know that you're interested in a different path.

Some students decide to take a year or two off after high school. Taking the time you need to figure things out is okay. Exploring different paths and gaining real-world experience can help you make a well-informed decision that aligns with your goals and aspirations. Whether you pursue higher education right after college or take a totally different route, the most important thing is to consider what feels right for you.

CHAPTER TWO
Choosing a Degree

After high school, you'll have the opportunity to decide where your future will take you. If you decide that further education is the path for you, the next step is to choose a degree program at a college or university. Selecting a degree path is a little like picking out a bicycle. Maybe you need a racing bike that will take you to your destination as fast as possible. Or you might be looking for an off-road bike that can take you on an adventure. Or it might be a better financial move to get a cheaper bike with the same great features of a brand-name bike but without the brand name. Just like there are different types of bikes for different types of cyclists, there are degree options for every type of student.

From associate's and bachelor's degree programs to trade and technical schools, there's something out there for all career paths and financial backgrounds. Think about where you want to be in the future. Which of these programs sounds like it will get you to your destination?

Skilled trade jobs are in high demand. As of 2022, there were more than 7,500 trade and technical schools in the US.

Associate's Degree Program

Associate's degrees give you a strong foundation in a specific field of study, such as nursing, marketing, information technology, and automotive technology. They usually take about two years to complete, but it can vary based on the program. You can find these programs at community colleges and technical schools. They can prepare you for entry-level jobs in your chosen field or act as a stepping stone to a bachelor's degree. Some associate's degrees also allow you to transfer credits to a bachelor's program.

Bachelor's Degree Program

Bachelor's degrees provide extensive and in-depth study, usually with a focus on one or two subjects. They typically take four years to finish, but there are many options to accelerate or extend the time to complete your degree. Colleges and universities offer bachelor's degrees, which come in several types based on the nature of the study. For instance, a Bachelor of Arts (BA) typically covers disciplines in the arts, humanities, and some social sciences. A Bachelor of Science (BS) focuses on technical or hard sciences, like biology or chemistry. A Bachelor of Fine Arts (BFA) is geared toward more practical and experiential study in areas such as painting, theater, or film. Each degree is designed to cover a broad range of subjects while also providing specialized knowledge and skills in its respective domain.

Trade and Technical Schools

Trade and technical schools offer an alternative to traditional colleges. They focus on hands-on learning and help you enter the workforce faster. Here are some examples of specialized training you can find at these schools:

- *Automotive Technology:* In this program, you'll learn about car repair, maintenance, and diagnostics. This is a good choice for people who like working with machines since you'll get hands-on experience working with engines, electrical systems, brakes, and more.

- *Construction and Carpentry:* These programs teach carpentry, plumbing, and electrical work for careers in construction and building repair.
- *Welding:* Welding is an in-demand skill in many different industries. This program will teach you how to join metal parts together. You'll study welding techniques and work with different metals.
- *Culinary Arts:* Do you love to cook? A culinary arts program will teach you professional cooking skills such as food preparation, menu planning, and kitchen management.
- *Electrical and Electronics:* If you love taking things apart to see how they work, this might be the program for you. You'll learn about electrical components and systems and how to fix them.
- *Healthcare Professions:* Although you can also study medicine at a university, many medical professionals are taught at technical schools, such as medical assistants, dental hygienists, nurses, and more.
- *Cosmetology:* If you're creative and artistic, this might be the field for you. You'll learn about hairstyling, cosmetics application, skin care, and salon management.

Factors to Consider in Choosing a Degree

As you think about your future education goals, consider the factors listed in Table 2. Which degree seems like the best fit for you?

Table 2. Factors to Consider in Choosing a Degree			
Factors to Consider	Associate's Degree	Bachelor's Degree	Trade/Technical School
Duration	About two years	About four years	A few months to two years
Cost	Lower tuition	Higher tuition	Lower tuition
Career Opportunities	Specialized roles including information technology and nursing	Wider range of industries	Skilled trades such as carpentry, plumbing, and construction
Job Market Demand	Entry-level positions	Often required in business or academic fields	High-demand trade positions
Transferability	Credits may transfer toward a bachelor's degree	Foundation for advanced studies, such as Masters or Doctorate degrees	Skills directly applicable to trade careers
Networking and Credibility	University networking opportunities	University networking opportunities	Industry-specific certifications

Every degree has its own benefits, so choose the path that aligns best with your individual preferences, career goals, financial situation, and learning style.

A Run-Down on Degrees

1. *High School Diploma:* Getting your high school diploma or GED will allow you to earn more money on average than those without a diploma. However, some jobs may require a college degree, and you might not make as much money or get promoted as easily as someone with more education.

2. *Associate's Degree:* People with associate's degrees often earn more than those with only a high school diploma or GED. Once you have an associate's degree, you'll know specialized information and skills that can lead to specific job opportunities.

3. *Bachelor's Degree:* Having a bachelor's degree can help you earn a much higher salary. With the in-depth knowledge you learn from this, more professional opportunities will be available to you.

4. *Master's Degree:* A master's degree is an advanced degree to further specialize after earning a bachelor's degree. Some people get their master's degree straight after graduating from university. Others wait to enroll in a program until they're looking to change careers or get a promotion.

5. *Doctorate (PhD):* A PhD is the highest degree you can get in many fields. To enter a PhD program, you'll likely need a bachelor's degree and possibly a master's degree too. These programs can take up to seven years to complete.

6. *Doctor of Medicine (MD):* An MD is a special kind of doctorate that medical doctors earn. Before earning their MD, many future doctors earn a bachelor's degree in a related field, such as biology or chemistry.

CHAPTER THREE
Paying for School

E ducation after high school may not be the right option for everyone. But if you do find yourself ready and able to enroll in further learning, it can open many exciting opportunities for you to grow in your career and as a person. As Nelson Mandela, former president of South Africa, once said, "Education is the most powerful weapon which you can use to change the world."

Unfortunately, college costs have been rising for many years. You might need some financial help to make this goal a reality. There are many options for funding your education, from loans and work-study programs to grants and scholarships. It's important to choose the option that makes the most sense for you.

Imagine you're really into cars, and you know how important it is to keep them running smoothly. Deciding how to pay for college is kind of like deciding what kind of car to buy. It's a smart move to invest in a good degree from the start, just as buying a car that runs well will help you avoid spending money in the future to fix major problems.

Many students have campus jobs while in college. These can include serving as an assistant to a professor or working as a computer lab attendant.

But if you never drive that car or do basic maintenance on it, the car will likely develop problems anyway. That can cost you even more money. Similarly, spending a ton of money on a degree without going to class won't give you a great return on your investment. You may not be able to finish your degree if your grades are too low, and even if you do, you won't have gained the knowledge or skills that would have helped you in your future endeavors. If you decide to get a degree of any kind, make sure you get the most out of it.

As you research options to help you pay for your degree, watch out for predatory loans. These are loans that give you a lot of money up front. This might sound tempting, but these loans charge you ultra-high interest rates later on. Many people get into more debt than they can handle because of these loans. Luckily, there are many other options available to prospective college students.

Different Types of Student Loans

Student loans are money that students can borrow to pay for higher education. There are many types of student loans available. It's important to understand how each works before deciding which is right for your needs.

Federal Student Loans

These loans are provided by the US Department of Education to support students in paying for their education. They have fixed interest rates, which means the interest remains the same throughout the repayment period, making it easier to plan and budget payments. There are four main types of federal student loans:

- *Direct Subsidized Loans:* These are based on financial need, and the government covers the interest while you're in school and during certain periods.
- *Direct Unsubsidized Loans:* Available to both undergraduate and graduate students, these loans can be used for educational expenses. They don't need you to demonstrate financial need.

FAFSA stands for Free Application for Federal Student Aid. Whether you're planning to attend a trade school or a four-year college, you and your family should fill out the FAFSA.

This means that you can qualify for this loan regardless of your income or financial situation.

- *Direct PLUS Loans:* These loans are available to graduate or professional students. The borrower is responsible for repaying the loan and any accrued interest.
- *Direct Consolidation Loans:* If you have multiple federal student loans, you can combine them into one loan for simpler repayment. This allows you to make one monthly payment and can provide beneficial repayment terms.

Federal student loans often have many benefits for repayment. Some of these include:

- *Deferment:* temporarily pauses payments due to specific conditions like unemployment
- *Forbearance:* halts or reduces payments, but interest may still accumulate

- *Forgiveness:* programs that can eliminate debt after meeting certain criteria, such as working in public service roles

Private Student Loans

These loans are from private companies, not the federal government. They can be an option if you need extra money for college after using scholarships, grants, and federal loans. But be careful, as they often have higher interest rates and fewer repayment choices.

Comparing Federal and Private Student Loans

Federal and private student loans both have many pros and cons. Knowing these distinctions will help you choose the loan that best fits your financial needs and long-term goals.

	Federal Student Loans	Private Student Loans
Interest Rates	Offer fixed interest rates	Offer fixed or variable rates
Repayment Options	Offer various repayment plans, including income-driven plans, and options for deferment, forbearance, or forgiveness	May have fewer repayment options and less flexibility in terms of deferment or forbearance
Loan Forgiveness and Discharge	May be discharged under certain circumstances, such as permanent disability or death	May be discharged under certain circumstances, such as permanent disability or death

- *Bank Loans:* These are offered by traditional banks. Interest rates and terms vary based on your credit history. You might need a cosigner, a person who agrees to take on the shared responsibility for the loan, if you have limited credit or a low credit score. Consider these loans only after exploring other options.
- *Credit Union Loans:* These are offered by nonprofit credit unions. They may have better terms and lower interest rates than bank loans. A cosigner might be required if you have limited credit or a low credit score.
- *Private Lender Loans:* These lenders specialize in educational loans. Rates and terms vary based on the lender and your credit history. You might need a cosigner, just like with bank and credit union loans. Some private lenders might offer unique benefits, such as lower interest rates for excellent academic performance. But remember to look into federal loans and other private lending options before relying on this type of loan.

Applying for Federal Student Loans

The FAFSA, short for Free Application for Federal Student Aid, is a form that high school students can fill out to apply for financial aid from the government. To qualify for federal student aid through the FAFSA, you must meet specific requirements and follow the application process. Colleges and the government will receive your application and determine how much money you're eligible to receive. You may want to ask a parent, teacher, or school counselor for help filling out the FAFSA to make sure you complete everything correctly and on time.

Upon submitting the FAFSA form and gaining acceptance into a college or university, you'll receive financial award letters detailing your eligible aid. This can include grants (money you don't have to repay, often based on need), scholarships (funds awarded for academic or extracurricular merit), work-study programs (opportunities to earn money through campus jobs), and loans.

FAFSA Eligibility Criteria

To qualify for federal student aid through the FAFSA, you must meet specific requirements, including:

1. Be a US citizen or an eligible non-citizen.
2. Have a valid Social Security number.
3. Enroll or get accepted in an eligible degree or certificate program at a qualifying institution.
4. Maintain satisfactory academic progress in college (good grades).

You'll also need to submit an Expected Family Contribution (EFC). The EFC measures your family's financial strength based on information in your FAFSA. It considers several factors, including income, assets, family size, and the number of family members attending college, determining your eligibility for need-based financial aid.

The Application Process

To apply for federal student aid through the FAFSA, you'll need to follow these steps:

1. Gather necessary documents such as tax returns, W-2 forms, and Social Security numbers.
2. Create a Federal Student Aid (FSA) ID, which is an electronic signature and provides access to online resources.
3. Complete the FAFSA form online or through the myStudentAid mobile app. The application will require financial and personal information.
4. List all the potential colleges and universities you wish to receive your financial aid information.
5. Meet state and college-specific deadlines to maximize your aid consideration.

Education Grants

Education grants are financial awards provided to students to cover educational costs, typically based on need, without the obligation of repayment. There are five main types of education grants available.

1. *Pell Grants:* Need-based grants by the federal government for undergraduate students with significant financial need.
2. *Federal Supplemental Educational Opportunity Grants (FSEOG):* For undergraduates with exceptional financial need, awarded on a first-come, first-served basis due to limited funds.

3. *Teacher Education Assistance for College and Higher Education (TEACH) Grants:* Available to students planning to teach in high-need fields at low-income schools, with teaching requirements to avoid turning the grant into a loan.
4. *State Grants:* Many states offer their grant programs to residents attending in-state institutions. Eligibility and application processes vary, so check your state's Department of Education for more information.
5. *Institutional Grants:* Colleges and universities may provide their own grants based on financial need, academic achievement, or other factors. Contact your school's financial aid office for application details

Scholarships

Scholarships are monetary awards given to students based on merit, talent, or other criteria, reducing the cost of their education. They do not require repayment. There are many different types of scholarships students can apply for.

1. *Merit-based Scholarships:* Awarded based on academic achievements, leadership qualities, or other talents. Provided by colleges, universities, private organizations, or the government. To apply, maintain a high grade point average (GPA), demonstrate exceptional talent, or showcase outstanding leadership skills.
2. *Need-based Scholarships:* Awarded based on financial need. Provided by the federal

Learning that you've been awarded a grant or scholarship to help pay for college is an exciting moment for both you and your family.

government, state governments, or the college/ university. Apply by completing the FAFSA.

3. *Athletic Scholarships:* Awarded to student–athletes who excel in a particular sport. Offered by colleges/universities with competitive athletic programs. Participate at a high level in your sport, network with college coaches, create a sports résumé or highlight reel, and research athletic programs at colleges of interest.

4. *Scholarships for Minorities and Underrepresented Groups:* Aim to provide educational opportunities to historically underrepresented groups, including racial and ethnic minorities, women, LGBTQ+ students, and students with disabilities. Apply by identifying as a member of a group and demonstrating financial need, academic achievement, or other qualifications.

Work-Study

The Federal Work–Study (FWS) program provides part-time jobs for undergraduate students with financial needs. A work-study program allows students to earn money to help pay for education expenses such as tuition and classroom materials.

Applying for Private Student Loans

If you don't get enough financial assistance through federal loans, grants, or school scholarships, you might think about getting private loans. But before you make this decision, there are some things you should keep in mind.

- *Creditworthiness and cosigners:* Private lenders look at your credit history to decide if they'll give you a loan. If you don't have much credit history or a good credit score, you can have someone else with good credit (like a parent or guardian) cosign the loan. This makes it more likely that you'll get approved, and you might get better interest rates and loan terms.
- *Shop around for the best rates and terms:* Check out different lenders, such as banks and credit unions. Look at their interest rates, how long you have before you must repay the loan, and what options they offer for repaying the money. Doing this research helps you make a smart decision that fits your financial situation and plans. You can use online tools and resources to make this process easier and find the best options.

Pros and Cons of Work-Study and Part-Time Jobs

The table below highlights the pros and cons of both work-study programs and part-time jobs:

	Work-Study Programs	Part-Time Jobs
Pros	Earn money for education	Offer an opportunity to earn your own money
	Flexible work hours	Gain real-world experience and valuable skills
	Relevant to studies/career	Interact with diverse groups of people
Cons	Limited positions available	Working alongside studies can be tough
	Earnings may be limited	Balancing work and study can lead to fatigue
	Limited field/position options	Part-time job may not align with career plans

Smart Ways to Borrow for College

When borrowing money for college, keep in mind that with most financial aid sources you will eventually need to pay the money back with interest. Making informed decisions can save you from future financial stress. Here are some tips to help you borrow wisely and reduce the burden of student loans.

35

Estimate Future Earnings

Before you borrow, think about how much money you might make after college. Research the job market, salaries in your chosen field, and opportunities for career growth. This will help you figure out how much to borrow and if you can pay it back comfortably after you finish your degree.

Explore Other Funding Sources

Reduce the amount you need to borrow by exploring other ways to get money for college. Scholarships and grants are great options because they give you free money for your studies without the expectation of repayment. Look for scholarships and grants that match your talents, interests, and background. Work-study programs offer part-time jobs on campus or in your community, helping you earn money for your education.

Borrow Only What You Need

Use your loan wisely for essential college expenses, including tuition, books, and living costs. Avoid using it for nonessential things such as vacations, TVs, or video games.

Keep Track of Loans

Keep a record of all your loans, including their terms and repayment plans. Know when you need to start repaying and what your options are. Being organized will help you manage your finances better.

Repayment Options and Strategies

When it's time to repay your loans, you'll have different options for both federal and private loans. Make sure you choose a strategy that fits your lifestyle, budget, and goals.

Federal Loan Repayment Plans

- *Standard Repayment Plans:* You pay a fixed amount every month for 10 years. This is a straightforward plan that helps you pay off your loans in a reasonable time.
- *Graduated Repayment Plans:* You start with lower monthly payments that increase every two years. This plan is good if your income is expected to go up over time, giving you flexibility in the beginning but higher payments later.
- *Extended Repayment Plans:* You get more time to pay, usually up to 25 years. This means lower monthly payments, but you'll end up paying more interest in the long run.
- *Income-Driven Repayment (IDR) Plans:* These plans adjust your payments based on how much you earn and the size of your family.
- *Loan Forgiveness Programs:* These programs forgive part of your loan if you meet certain conditions, such as working in public service or teaching.

Private Loan Repayment Plans

When you borrow money from a private lender, how you pay it back can differ depending on the lender's rules. Here are some things to know:

- *Repayment Terms:* Each private loan comes with its own rules, including how long you have to

Tips for Successful Repayment

Here are some helpful tips to make paying back your loan easier and more successful:

- *Automatic Payments:* Set up automatic payments with your lender, so your monthly loan payment gets deducted from your bank account without you having to do anything.
- *Extra Payments and Prepayments:* If you're able to pay more than your monthly payment, and want to pay off your loans faster, you can ask your lender about these options.
- *Budgeting for Loan Payments:* Create a budget to manage your money wisely. It'll show you how much you can afford for loan payments while still taking care of other important expenses.

pay it back (usually 5 to 20 years) and whether the interest rate stays the same or changes over time. Fixed rates mean your monthly payments will stay the same, while variable rates might go up or down.

- *School-Payment Options:* Some private lenders offer choices while you're still in school. You might be able to make smaller payments (interest-only) or no payments at all (deferred) until you finish school.

Combining Loans and Getting Better Terms

When you have many loans, there are ways to make paying them back easier or get better deals.

- *Federal Direct Consolidation Loan:* If you have multiple federal loans, you can merge them into one with a Federal Direct Consolidation Loan. That means you'll make only one payment each month. While this might make the overall interest costs a bit higher, it can be a good option if you want simplicity without losing federal loan benefits.
- *Private Loan Refinancing:* Private loan refinancing means you replace one or more of your existing loans, whether private or federal, with a new loan from a private lender. This could get you a lower interest rate or change the repayment time, making your monthly payments lower. But before you decide, you should do your research. You might need someone to cosign with you to get better terms. And if you refinance federal loans with a private lender, you might lose federal loan benefits.

Paying for school can be challenging, but it is also manageable. It's important to explore all of your options, including scholarships, grants, part-time jobs, and, when necessary, student loans. Planning ahead can help you avoid last-minute financial stress. Always be informed about the terms and responsibilities of any student loans you consider to ensure they align with your long-term financial goals. Remember, investing in your education is an investment in your future, so approach it with a positive attitude and a proactive mindset.

CHAPTER FOUR
Spending and Saving Money

Imagine you're planning your dream vacation. There's lots to plan, but before anything else, you'll need to figure out how to pay for it! First, you have to figure out how much the trip will cost. Then, you'll gather finances, save money, and carefully budget for all the expenses. Saving up for a big vacation is similar to preparing for college.

When planning for a vacation, you have to plan for different costs such as transportation, food, and hotels or other housing. College has similar costs. Of course, you'll need to pay tuition, but you'll also need to pay for class materials, including books, notebooks, and specific materials for certain classes. Art classes, for example, may require paints or pencils. Software coding classes may need specific computers and computer programs.

You'll also need to prepare to pay for food and housing, whether that means living in a college dorm, an apartment, or other space. You have to make sure you're in good financial shape for everything you'll need for classwork and life outside of school.

Tracking bills, daily costs, and college fees can help you avoid debt. Use a budgeting program or make a list to avoid surprise expenses.

Common College Expenses

While the costs of college can vary from person to person, here are some typical expenses for pursuing higher education.

Tuition Fees

Tuition is the money you pay for your college classes. How much tuition costs can vary depending on the college you choose, the program you're in, and whether you live in the same state as the college you attend. If you live in the same state as a public college, you might get a lower tuition rate called in-state tuition. But if you live in a different state, you'll probably have to pay the higher out-of-state tuition.

Private colleges usually have higher tuition fees compared to public universities. Public universities receive financial support from the state government, which helps them offer lower tuition rates, especially for students who live in the same state as the university. Private colleges rely on tuition and donors to pay their expenses.

College Living Expenses

- *Living in dorms:* When you live in a dorm, you usually pay for room and board, which includes your room and a meal plan. Dorm living costs vary depending on the college or university, the kind of dorm, and any other services supplied. Living with other students in a dorm can enhance your college experience. Plus, your dorm might have amenities like internet access, laundry facilities, study lounges, fitness centers, and social events where you can meet new people.
- *Living in an apartment:* Some students prefer to live off-campus in a private apartment. You'll need to budget for monthly rent if you live in an apartment. When looking for an apartment, make sure the rent fits within your budget. You'll also need to budget for utilities and food. Utilities often consist of electricity, water, gas, and sometimes extra services such as internet or garbage collection.
- *Living at home:* Some people enroll in a college near their hometown. This gives them a chance to continue living with their parents or guardians. In some situations, this can help save money on housing and utilities. Meals might be provided at home, saving money on meal plans as well.

Books and Supplies

You'll need to budget for textbooks, study materials, and other supplies for your classes. If you're in a specialized program, you might also need specific materials, such as art supplies for art degrees, scrubs or stethoscopes for medical programs, tools for vocational certifications, and cameras for photography degrees. Look for ways to save money to help you manage these costs. Buying used books or renting supplies are just a few examples.

Transportation

Getting to and from college costs money. There will be costs connected with commuting, whether you take public transportation, drive, or bike to school. When calculating your budget, don't forget to account for expenses such as gas, parking costs, and transit passes.

Personal Expenses

You'll also need to plan for everyday expenses such as clothing, toiletries, entertainment, and insurance. These little things can add up over time. Keep track of your spending and include it in your budget.

Putting It All Together

Learning to balance spending and saving money in college is a crucial life skill. By creating a budget, seeking out ways to save money, and prioritizing your needs over wants, you can make the most of your financial resources. Remember, the habits you develop in college regarding money management will lay the groundwork for your financial health in the future.

CHAPTER FIVE
Career Planning

Starting a career is like embarking on an exciting journey through an unfamiliar land. You might encounter crossroads or roadblocks or stumble upon discoveries that lead you to change course. Like any good explorer, you'll need a compass and a map to help you find your way. Your short-term and long-term goals serve as your compass, providing direction amid the ever-changing landscape of your career journey. A detailed career plan acts as your map, showing your path forward. From time to time, you may need to change course. Many people shift jobs and even pivot careers multiple times throughout their lives. Understanding and regularly revisiting your career plan can help you navigate these transitions, ensuring you remain on track to reach your long-term goals.

You can start exploring what you want to do for school or work while you are still in high school, but you should check back in with yourself every so often to make sure you're still on the path that's right for you. It's fine if your career objectives shift over time. Stay open-minded and

Even if you love your job, keep your mind open to new possibilities. You might start out working in a skilled trade but eventually teach others how to do your job.

look for opportunities to grow. When exploring the many opportunities available to you, think about what the former Apple CEO Steve Jobs said: "Your work is going to fill a large part of your life, and the only way to be truly satisfied is to do what you believe is great work. And the only way to do great work is to love what you do."

Career planning is an ongoing process that empowers you to continuously shape your future. Once you start working in one job, you might get wrapped up in day-to-day life and forget to keep working toward your larger goals. For example, in a project management role, you could become so focused on organizing team meetings and managing deadlines that you lose sight of your personal growth and long-term career objectives. Revisiting your short-term and long-term goals will help you keep those goals in your sights while still enjoying the journey.

Long-Term Goals

Long-term career planning goals are the big dreams and ambitions you have for your career. These can take 5 to 10 years, or even longer, to achieve. Some examples of long-term goals are aiming for a specific high-level job, such as becoming a boss or leader in your field, switching to a completely different job you're more passionate about, or having a good balance between your work and personal life.

To set realistic long-term goals, make sure your goals align with what you really care about and want for your future. Return to the self-assessment you completed earlier and keep it in mind as you write down your career goals. Then, break these big goals into smaller, achievable steps so you can track your progress and adjust when needed. Get in the habit of returning to these goals and deciding if they still work for you. Remember, it's okay to change your goals as you learn, grow, and change.

Short-Term Goals

Short-term goals are things you want to achieve in the near future, likely in the next one to three years. Setting short-term goals allows you to break down your larger career vision into manageable chunks, making it easier to stay focused and motivated. One of your first short-term goals might be getting an internship or entry-level position in a certain field. Or maybe your goal is to complete job training or higher education in a certain amount of time.

Creating a Career Road Map

Your career journey needs a road map to help guide you through your process. Imagine where you want to be in the future and chart out your career path accordingly. You can do this on a computer or write it down on a piece of paper. Identify what things you'll use to measure your progress along the way. These might include job titles, certifications, or salary markers that you want to achieve.

Adjust Goals as Needed

As time goes on, your priorities and wants might change. The goals you set at 18 might not fit who you are at 35. Life is dynamic, and circumstances may change. The perfect job for you might not even exist yet! Regularly reassess your goals to ensure they continue to align with your values, passions, and overall career road map. Be prepared to be flexible as your personal life and the job market evolve.

Seek Guidance and Support

You don't have to do this alone! In fact, it'd be almost impossible to meet all your goals without asking for help. Ask for guidance from mentors, career counselors, and experienced individuals in your field who can offer insights and share their career experiences. Joining industry associations and professional organizations can help direct your career plan. These groups often offer networking events, workshops, and conferences where you can learn from industry experts and connect with peers.

S.M.A.R.T. Goal Setting Framework

SMART goals, defined by objectives that are Specific, Measurable, Achievable, Relevant, and Time-bound, offer a structured approach to setting achievable targets. They transform vague ambitions into clear, actionable steps, providing a road map for personal and professional growth. The measurability and time-bound nature of SMART goals also help ongoing progress tracking and adjustment, providing motivation and a sense of accomplishment.

Specific: Instead of saying, "Improve my communication skills," a specific goal could be, "Attend a public speaking course to enhance my presentation skills."

Measurable: If your goal is to increase your professional network, you can set a measurable goal by attending at least two monthly networking events.

Achievable: Your objectives should be realistic and attainable, given your resources, abilities, and situations. Setting attainable goals guarantees that you are on the right track and avoids setting yourself up for failure.

Relevant: If you're aiming for career advancement, setting a relevant goal could be, "Complete a leadership development program to enhance my managerial skills."

Time-bound: If you want to start a side business, you could set a time-bound goal by saying, "Launch my online store within six months."

Financial Goals and Smart Money Moves

In addition to your career goals, it's a good practice to list some financial goals and set a budget that matches them. Do you want to have your student loans paid off by a certain date? Maybe you want to be making a certain salary by a specific point in your career. While money isn't the only factor in planning your life after high school, it can be an important one to consider.

Why Watch Your Spending:

- *Avoid Overspending:* Keep track of where your money goes to avoid getting into unnecessary debt.
- *Focus on Education:* Make sure your loan funds cover important stuff like tuition, books, and supplies.
- *Build Good Money Skills:* Learning to manage money now sets you up for success later.

Tips for Smart Spending:

- *Budgeting Basics:* Plan your spending on school, living, and fun. Be smart about it.
- *Use Money Apps:* Apps can help you keep an eye on your money and find ways to save.
- *Know about Interest:* Understand how interest works with loans and make smart borrowing choices.

Ways to Cut College Costs:

- *Picking the Right College:* Think about community colleges, state schools, or online classes for lower costs.
- *Saving on Housing and Food:* Share housing, cook meals, or pick a smaller meal plan to save money.
- *Book Smarts:* Rent or buy used textbooks, and look online for free educational stuff.
- *Scholarships and Grants:* Free money! Look for ones that match your studies.

Use Loans Wisely:

Borrow only what you really need. Less debt later is a good thing.

Overcoming Obstacles and Achieving Success

Imagine your journey through education and career planning like a challenging hike through the mountains. As you set out, you encounter steep hills, unexpected twists and turns, and tough weather that will put your skills to the test. But you'll also come across breathtaking nature, meet new friends, and feel incredibly accomplished.

Just like a tough hike, life after high school will bring unexpected obstacles and challenges that you need to overcome before you reach your goals. Skills such as planning, perseverance, and self-awareness will help you make it to the summit!

Common Challenges and How to Overcome Them

Starting your life after high school is exciting, but it can be tough if you're not prepared when obstacles appear. Let's review some common challenges and how you might deal with them to keep moving forward.

- *Academic challenges:* College or trade school education can feel very different from high school classes! You'll have much more freedom to balance your academic responsibilities and extracurricular commitments. Plan your schedule wisely, prioritize schoolwork, and practice effective time management. Even if you're not struggling, be proactive by asking for support from teachers, tutors, or study groups.
- *Career challenges:* The transition from high school to the professional world is a big shift, bringing a new set of responsibilities and expectations. You'll find that managing work tasks, team collaborations, and maintaining a healthy work–life balance takes some care and practice. Try to plan ahead. Prioritize your responsibilities, refine your organizational skills, and don't hesitate to seek guidance from experienced colleagues or mentors. Even when things are going smoothly, building a support network and seeking professional development opportunities can set the stage for long-term success and job satisfaction.

- *Financial barriers:* Pursuing education after high school and stepping into your chosen career path can both pose significant financial challenges. To navigate these, it's crucial to explore all available financial aid options, such as scholarships, grants, and work-study programs, as well as seek guidance on career-specific funding opportunities. It is essential to adopt a budget-friendly approach by tracking your expenses and identifying cost-cutting strategies. This might include renting textbooks, sharing living spaces with roommates, or opting for part-time work to supplement your income. Establishing a solid financial foundation not only aids in overcoming educational costs but also lays the groundwork for a stable financial future as you progress in your career.
- *Personal and emotional difficulties:* There are tons of life transitions that come after high school, such as moving to a new city, living on your own, and meeting new people. Seek support from friends, family, coworkers, or campus resources to make the most of your experience and take care of yourself. Be open to seeking professional help if you need it.

Strategies to Overcome Obstacles
- *Self-reflection:* When you're faced with an issue, take some time to think about what's causing it. Ask yourself questions like, "Why is this happening?" or "What can I do differently to

solve this problem?" Brainstorm different ideas to solve the problem. You can make a pros and cons list to consider the good and bad sides of each solution.

- *Cultivate a growth mindset:* Remember that challenges can allow you to learn and grow. When things don't go as planned, try to learn from it and keep going. Take a moment to understand what went wrong and what you can learn from it.

- *Reach out for help:* It's okay to ask for help from friends, family, or teachers. Academic support services, such as tutoring, can also help address learning challenges and improve your performance. If you're facing stress, anxiety, or other mental health challenges, find a counselor or therapist who can help you through these feelings.

Tips for Sustainable Success

Your career and education are marathons, not sprints. Set up healthy habits now to reach your goals and fulfill your dreams.

- *Embrace lifelong learning:* The most successful people are always looking for opportunities to learn and grow. Attend workshops, seminars, or training sessions to enhance your skills and knowledge. Keep yourself informed about the latest trends and emerging technologies in your field. This will show potential employers that you are proactive and adaptable.

Monitoring Progress and Celebrating Success

It is important to track your growth and acknowledge accomplishments along the way. Look for practical ways to track your progress toward your goals.

- *Journaling:* Write down your goals, break them into actionable steps, and track your progress over time. Use your journal as a tool for self-reflection and self-motivation.
- *Using an app on your phone to track progress:* Goal-tracking apps can help you stay organized and monitor your progress. These apps allow you to set specific goals, track your daily or weekly progress, and receive reminders and notifications to keep you on track.
- *Adjust your plan as needed:* Consider what is functioning well and what may be improved. If specific techniques or activities are not producing the expected outcomes, be willing to make necessary changes.
- *Set milestones and markers along the way to recognize your accomplishments:* These milestones can include finishing a difficult course, receiving great feedback, or reaching a specific career milestone. Recognize your accomplishments and give yourself credit for reaching them.
- *Remind yourself of your goals and the wider picture:* Role models, success stories, and motivational slogans can all serve as sources of inspiration. Surround yourself with a supportive network of family, friends, or mentors who can offer advice and hold you accountable.

- *Be adaptable and resilient:* Life can be challenging at times. Stress and setbacks happen to everyone, so it's important to have coping strategies for when these things come up. Find healthy ways to manage stress, such as exercise, mindfulness, or talking to someone you trust. Don't get discouraged! Remember, setbacks are a part of life. As the former CEO of General Electric once said, "Face reality as it is, not as it was or as you wish it to be."
- *Monitor and celebrate progress and success:* Monitoring and celebrating progress will boost your morale and help you maintain focus on your goals. This can help motivate you to keep going even when you hit obstacles. These moments of celebration act as positive reinforcement and keep your goals at the front of your mind.

Career planning is an exciting journey that requires self-reflection, research, and adaptability. Start by identifying your interests and strengths. Set both short- and long-term goals, and don't be afraid to seek advice from mentors or counselors. Remember, your career path may evolve over time, so stay open to new opportunities and experiences that can help you grow both personally and professionally.

CONCLUSION
Let's Sum It All Up

Throughout this book, you've gained valuable insights and knowledge about high school diplomas, GED certificates, college degree programs, trade schools, financial aid, and other important aspects of planning for your life after high school. Now, it's time to put these insights into action!

Keep these points in mind as you plan and prepare for your academic or professional career:

- Remember that education is not one-size-fits-all. Take time to think about what motivates you and what you want for your future.
- Set short-term and long-term goals. Break bigger goals down into actionable SMART goals and create a plan to achieve them.
- Be financially savvy. Look into financial aid, scholarship, and budgeting options to help you achieve your educational goals.

- Keep exploring new fields and industries even after you've started your educational journey. Career exploration is a lifelong process, so seek internships, volunteer opportunities, and extracurricular activities that align with your interests.
- Don't forget to pat yourself on the back along the way! Surround yourself with a strong network of friends, family, and mentors who will celebrate your wins with you.

As you apply the skills and knowledge gained from this book, remember that your future is in your hands. You have the power to shape your education and career path, to pursue your passions, and to make a meaningful impact on the world.

Use the tools you've gained in this book and seize the opportunities that lie ahead of you. Reflect on your passions and skills, stay curious, and never stop learning. Endless possibilities await you!

GLOSSARY

apprenticeship: a training program where individuals learn a skill or trade from an experienced person, like a mentor

associate's degree: a two-year college degree that can be earned after high school, providing basic knowledge in a specific subject

bachelor's degree: a four-year college degree that can be earned after high school, signifying completion of a more comprehensive study in a specific field

career path: the route or journey individuals take in their chosen career, including the jobs and experiences gained along the way

college: a place of higher education where individuals can attend classes after high school to earn a degree

community college: a college that offers two-year programs and is often more affordable than traditional four-year colleges

cosigner: a person who agrees to take on the shared responsibility for repaying a loan or debt if the primary borrower fails to make the required payments

deferment: a temporary pause to payments due to specific conditions like unemployment

dual enrollment: a program that allows high school students to take college courses for credit while still in high school

extracurricular activities: activities outside of regular classes, including clubs, sports, or volunteering, that individuals can join in school

FAFSA (Free Application for Federal Student Aid): a form individuals fill out to see if they're eligible for financial help to pay for college

financial aid: assistance or money given to help individuals pay for college

forbearance: a temporary break from paying back a loan, usually when facing financial difficulties

grade point average (GPA): the average of grades in all classes, usually on a scale of 0 to 4

internship: a short-term job experience that helps individuals learn and gain skills in a particular field

loan forgiveness: programs that can eliminate debt after meeting certain criteria, such as working in public service roles

master's degree: an advanced degree individuals can earn after completing a bachelor's degree

mentor: an experienced person who guides and supports individuals in their education or career

networking: building relationships for education, employment, or business

résumé: a document that lists education, work experience, and skills when applying for a job

return on investment: a measure of how much value or benefit is gained from an investment, like education

scholarship: money given to help pay for college, usually based on academic or athletic achievement

student loan: money borrowed to pay for college, which must be repaid later with interest

trade school: a school that provides specific training and skills for a particular job or trade

university: a place of higher education that offers facilities for teaching and research

SOURCE NOTES

8   "An investment in . . . the best interest." Franklin, Benjamin. (1757). *The Way to Wealth*. B. Franklin and D. Hall. 1757

24   " . . . education is the . . . to change the world." Mandela, Nelson. (2003). Lighting Your Way to a Better Future. Speech delivered at the launch of Mindset Network, Johannesburg, South Africa.

45   "Your work is going to fill. . . what you do." Jobs, Steve. (2005). Commencement address at Stanford University, Palo Alto, CA.

55   "Face reality as . . . it to be." Welch, Jack., & Byrne, John. A. (2001). *Jack: Straight from the Gut*. New York: Warner Business Books.

SELECTED BIBLIOGRAPHY

Burnett, Bill, and Dave Evans. *Designing Your Life: How to Build a Well-Lived, Joyful Life.* New York: Knopf, 2016.

Clark, Dorie. *The Long Game: How to Be a Long-Term Thinker in a Short-Term World.* Boston, MA: Harvard Business Review Press, 2021.

Goldsmith, Marshall. *What Got You Here Won't Get You There.* New York: McGraw-Hill, 2012.

Harris, Carla A. *Expect to Win: Proven Strategies for Success from a Wall Street Vet.* New York: Hudson Street Press, 2009.

Oneal, Anthony, Rachel Cruze, and Dave Ramsey. *The Graduate Survival Guide: 5 Mistakes You Can't Afford to Make in College.* Brentwood, TN: Ramsey Press, The Lampo Group, LLC, 2017.

Peterson's. *Teens' Guide to College & Career Planning 11th Edition.* Peterson's, 2012.

This Is Your Life: A Career and Education Planning Guide. Edmonton, Alberta: Enterprise & Advanced Education, 2012.

Whyte, Iain Boyd. *Man-Made Future: Planning, Education, and Design in Mid-Twentieth Century Britain.* London: Routledge, 2007.

FURTHER READING

Books

The Careers Handbook: The Ultimate Guide to Planning Your Future.
London: Dorling Kindersley Ltd, 2022.
A comprehensive guide designed to help readers plan their future careers. Offering expert advice and practical insights, this book covers various aspects of career planning, from exploring interests to résumé writing and interview tips. With its user-friendly approach, it equips individuals with the necessary tools to make informed decisions and pursue a successful and fulfilling career path.

Christen, Carol, and Richard N. Bolles. *What Color Is Your Parachute? For Teens: Discovering Yourself, Defining Your Future.* Berkeley: Ten Speed Press, 2015.
A comprehensive guide for young individuals taking the first step in their journey toward employment. With an emphasis on identifying unique skills and passions, it provides practical exercises and valuable insights to help teens navigate the complexities of choosing a career path. Engaging and relevant, this manual equips young readers with the tools they need to understand the job market, make informed decisions about their future, and find a sense of personal and professional satisfaction.

The Princeton Review, and Robert Franek. *College Admission 101, 3rd Edition.* Framingham, MA: Princeton Review, 2022.
A trusted resource co-authored by The Princeton Review and Robert Franek, this book offers essential guidance on the college admission process. From selecting the right colleges to preparing standout applications, it provides valuable tips and strategies to increase the chances of getting into the desired institutions and starting a successful academic journey.

The Princeton Review, and Kalman Chany. *Paying for College, 2023.* Framingham, MA: Princeton Review, 2022.
This book offers a comprehensive guide to understanding and managing the costs of higher education. Each new edition provides up-to-date information on scholarships, financial aid, and other funding options. By equipping students and their families with valuable financial planning tools, it helps them make informed decisions about financing college education without overwhelming debt.

Websites

CareerOneStop

> https://www.careeronestop.org
> CareerOneStop is a site sponsored by the US Department of Labor. You can access various self-assessments to help you identify the kind of work that matches your skills and interests. The site outlines the steps to make SMART career goals and provides a directory of local help you can connect with, whether a job center or employment and training programs.

Career Project

> https://www.thecareerproject.org
> Career Project is a site with various tools to help schools, career changers, and students navigate their future employment. You can learn about different careers by reviewing their career guides and job profiles.

College Insight

> https://www.college-insight.org
> College Insight provides expert college admissions guidance, strategy, and mentoring in a personalized and inclusive manner. Their goal is to ensure academic, career, and financial success for all the students.

Federal Student Aid

> https://studentaid.gov
> Federal Student Aid is the largest provider of financial aid for college in the US Department of Education. They make college education possible for more than 10 million students each year. Federal Student Aid is responsible for managing the student financial assistance programs authorized under Title IV of the Higher Education Act of 1965.

Mapping Your Future

> https://www.mappingyourfuture.org
> Mapping Your Future is a site for students getting prepared for post-secondary school. The site helps students achieve academic success by including access to financial aid professionals, high school counselors, and resources for parents and families of students.

INDEX

ABOUT THE AUTHOR

Dr. Nicholas Suivski is a finance, business, and phonics writer with an entrepreneurial spirit. He has owned multiple businesses and is a practicing doctor of physical therapy. Now, he focuses on writing and business development roles. Past books he has written include *Defining Money in the Age of Cryptocurrency, Investing with Cryptocurrency: How to Buy, Sell, and Save, The Future of Cryptocurrency*, and *Scholarly Jim*. When Nicholas is not writing and working, he enjoys snowboarding, hiking, soccer, and driving cars.

PHOTO ACKNOWLEDGMENTS